T0209422

I Am More Than Me

A Self-Help Junkie's Journal To Surrender

Jocelyn Esther Nelson

BALBOA.PRESS

A DIVISION OF HAY HOUSE

Balboa Press books may be ordered through booksellers or by contacting:

Balboa Press
A Division of Hay House
1663 Liberty Drive
Bloomington, IN 47403
www.balboapress.com
1 (877) 407-4847

Because of the dynamic nature of the Internet, any web addresses or links contained in this book may have changed since publication and may no longer be valid. The views expressed in this work are solely those of the author and do not necessarily reflect the views of the publisher, and the publisher hereby disclaims any responsibility for them.

The author of this book does not dispense medical advice or prescribe the use of any technique as a form of treatment for physical, emotional, or medical problems without the advice of a physician, either directly or indirectly. The intent of the author is only to offer information of a general nature to help you in your quest for emotional and spiritual well-being. In the event you use any of the information in this book for yourself, which is your constitutional right, the author and the publisher assume no responsibility for your actions.

Any people depicted in stock imagery provided by Getty Images are models,
and such images are being used for illustrative purposes only.
Certain stock imagery © Getty Images.

Photo by Daniel Tafjord on Unsplash

Scriptures taken from the King James Version of the bible

Print information available on the last page.

ISBN: 978-1-9822-4297-8 (sc)
ISBN: 978-1-9822-4298-5 (e)

Balboa Press rev. date: 02/19/2020

CONTENTS

"Creativity absolves criticism!" – Julia Cameron

INTRODUCTION

We all fantasize as children of who we want to become when we get older. I knew at a very young age that I wanted to tell stories. Whether it was through dance or performance, I loved capturing the essence of the rhythm with my body or finding the truth of a character. I was flexible, dramatic and I was really good at it! As cliché as it may sound, I dreamed that I was going to be a famous, award winning actor one day. I wished to be living in a fabulous mansion in sunny Hollywood, California sipping champagne with Robin Leach on the Lifestyles of the Rich and Famous. It could've happened, but it never did.

Mystically, you could've said that it wasn't in the stars for me. Maybe I should've been born a few days earlier under the Capricorn and that would have aligned the stars in making dreams come true. Or statistically, you could've said that being raised by a single mother with 7 children, in her mother's home, that it would be a total crap shoot coming from such a small blue collar town in New Jersey. Either way, I have released whatever reasons I've told myself as to why I've never achieved my childhood fantasy. As an adult, I am still very interested in helping others tell their stories. In doing so, I am impassioned in becoming the storyteller of my own life.

Let me begin by saying that I am not an expert. What you do with the information included in this workbook is completely up to you. There is a saying that you have to put at least 10,000 hours into "something" in order to be an expert in "it". My 10,000 hours over the last 2 decades of my life have been poured into self-help resources. So in this context, I'm an expert in helping myself. I will call myself an expert in me. You will become the expert of you.

Included are several pivotal experiences that led me to a deeper sense of self-awareness, self-acceptance and spirituality. In addition, the suggested books, along with my self-help practices are only that, suggestions. These processes are not to be taken as the only path to serenity. They are only a mere framework to guide you to become more curious in your own wellbeing practices, as well as an exploration into what moves you into your more-accepting self.

Please know that I am still exploring into my greater self and I am no greater than you for writing this book. My hope is that by sharing a few practices that I've learned along the way, they will inspire you to seek and find your own truth. Then, take it one step further and share it with others. Whether it's through therapy, an affirmation or even painting a picture. Just get to it!

To be honest, I just recently gave myself permission to share these events. First, they are emotional to recount and very personal to me. Second, I continued to tell myself that I had to wait until I became 'somebody' to be worthy to share. Well, I waited and waited. Years went by and I asked myself, "When will somebody tell me that it's time?" More years passed and then I asked myself, "Who is this somebody and when are they coming?" I'm here to tell you that they are not coming. This is a ridiculous thought. No one is going to roll out a big red carpet to give us permission to share our experiences. It is up to us to do the work and take the courage to share our truth.

I was fed up with waiting for the approval to become what or who I thought society considered a worthy person with worthy life experiences. You know, someone with over 1 million followers, celebrity status or a social media influencer. There is nothing wrong with having any of these statuses however, being what the world considers famous in order to share with each other, is definitely not a requirement. We don't even need to go viral! We just need the virtuous ability to be vulnerable and to tell our authentic story. Ironically, in sharing our unique experiences, we will find similarities with each other and moreover, empathy for each other's differences.

Are you like I was? Waiting for another person or some grandiose authority to give you permission to share the expression of your unique inner self. Regardless of the lack of proof that we can help anybody else by being whom we really are, no matter the title of our job and the salary that it brings or the amount of friends or likes that we receive on our social media posts, we do matter. Our personal journeys matter.

We've all experienced some form of struggle and we all want to fit in somewhere. I know for me, I never felt authentic trying to live up to what I thought were someone else's standards of who I should be. It was too hard for me to keep up with their expectations and honestly, it became exhausting trying to figure it all out. I wanted to check all their boxes in order to personally feel successful, happy and even beautiful. I understand that we all want to belong. But you tell me, if God made every one of our fingerprints unique, then why are we all trying to be like everyone else? It is time that we find out who we are and who we shall evolve to be. There is a soul inside of us that wants to be present in our world. Why not find out what that feels like?

Can you accept that you are perfectly imperfect? Do you believe that you can be your authentic self without the guilt and the self-condemnation? The intention of this journal is for you to scribe from your heart. Share all the good, the bad and the ugly of your journey. Can you hear your inner voice calling you? Stop and listen to it. It's your soul calling you out of your head and into your heart! Now, let's get it down on paper!

"The present moment is here for a reason. Don't argue with it. Accept it as if you have chosen it."

\- Eckhart Tolle

THE FIRST BREAK

It was 2007 and there I was, a 31-year old woman, curled up in a fetal position on the bathroom floor of my master bedroom. Sobbing uncontrollably. This was not the typical pity party that a young woman has in the wake of a minor disturbance. I didn't have a bad day at work because of a crappy boss. I wasn't struggling to pay my bills. I wasn't even having a bad hair day. Nothing was wrong and yet, in a short moment, absolutely everything went wrong.

There was an unforecasted storm forming inside of me. A tsunami of pain had collided with a fleeting moment of vulnerability and I truly didn't see it coming! It plainly knocked me off my feet and sent me into a soul stirring cry that I had never experienced before. I recall barely breathing in between the groans. The moans were only there to let me know that I was alive and breathing. This pain was very present and very real. It was not a dream.

My heart filled with such sadness that it weakened my knees and left me buckling down to the ground. I felt broken open. Broken, like an old terracotta pot, pushed to the floor by a thrust of wind and shattered into large pieces. Chunky-like. There, on the hard and unwelcoming marbled-tiled floor, were the large chunks of my so-called solid life. I was emotionally shattered.

After this uncontainable tantrum stopped, I stared into the dark puddle of my tears on the floor. What just happened? I could barely move. I wanted to jump up, wipe my face clean and get back to my busy day but the weight of my body had become so heavy that I was stuck to the floor. I was alone in my desperation. The sink would become my crutch to get myself off of the ground. Gripping the cold white porcelain tightly with my hands, I found enough strength to raise myself to my knees and then slowly to my feet.

I caught a glimpse of my reflection in the mirror and before quickly wiping away my tears in shame of this outpour, I stopped. At first glance, I didn't recognize myself. I was sure that it was my own reflection. After all, I was the only one in the room. The only one in the entire house. Not a single person, animal or house plant could have mistakenly been there. It was me! Alone and very exposed. It was as if I was looking at myself for the very first time. I immediately rationalized that the room was dark and thought my reflection was diminished due to the late afternoon sun, streaming from my bedroom window. It cast a shadow into the windowless room. I was still the self-proclaimed independent woman who was always self-assured. Yet, today I wasn't sure of who it was, that was looking back at me.

I stared.

I glared.

I observed.

I was mesmerized.

My eyes were very bright and brown and glowing with amber hues. Oddly enough, they were the same color as they'd always been. But this day, my eyes were bold. Suddenly, I heard a direct and firm voice say, I am more than me.

Who was that?

Did I just say that?

I am more than me?

I stood still in my solitude and I said it out loud this time. This time, with clarity. This time, with a new confidence. And then, at that moment, I knew exactly what it meant. Yes! I am more than me!

I became very quiet, very still and with the last residue of tears on my cheeks, it was very clear to me. This was a divine secret that had been revealed to me, by me. It sprung from somewhere deep down inside. A deep knowing. It was so as a matter of fact, that it startled me when it first came out of my mouth. In all of my adult years of living, I had been relentlessly striving to be this most improved version of myself and yet, my own soul comforted me in my fight with despair and fear of who I was becoming.

But like a good mortal, I pushed the brilliant epiphany aside. With no time to spare to embrace this enlightened moment, I picked up the pieces of my pain and somehow glued myself back together again. I was back to my self-professed, self-reliant existence. My quick bounce back would be only temporary. Regrettably, I had no idea that this would not be the last time that my life would be shattered on the bathroom floor.

"Your inner voice is your ready compass for when you let it lead you out of darkness, you trust its readiness to guide you surefootedly in troubled times."

– Doreen Virtue Ph.D.

If I am more than me, then you are more than you. Whether that's being a wife, mother, daughter, an employee and even employer, we're beyond the roles of cultural appropriation. We are beyond who others tell us we need to be, that includes biologically and socially.

Are you living too small in a certain aspect of your life? Are you struggling to live too large in another area?

Be honest with where your energy is going and how you may need to reallocate your time to stay on the best path to your authentic self. Please use the next pages to describe where you may need to expand your focus or what you might need to give up. Either way, you will be moving in the direction of your heart's center.

Journal Entry
Date:____

_____

_____

_____

_____

_____

_____

_____

_____

_____

_____

_____

_____

_____

_____

_____

_____

_____

_____

_____

Journal Entry
Date:___

_____

_____

_____

_____

_____

_____

_____

_____

_____

_____

_____

_____

_____

_____

_____

_____

_____

Journal Entry
Date:_____

_____

_____

_____

_____

_____

_____

_____

_____

_____

_____

_____

_____

_____

_____

_____

_____

_____

_____

_____

Journal Entry
Date:___

_____

_____

_____

_____

_____

_____

_____

_____

_____

_____

_____

_____

_____

_____

_____

_____

_____

_____

_____

_____

Journal Entry
Date:____

_____

_____

_____

_____

_____

_____

_____

_____

_____

_____

_____

_____

_____

_____

_____

_____

_____

_____

_____

_____

_____

Journal Entry
Date:____

_____

_____

_____

_____

_____

_____

_____

_____

_____

_____

_____

_____

_____

_____

_____

_____

_____

Journal Entry
Date:____

Journal Entry
Date:____

_____

_____

_____

_____

_____

_____

_____

_____

_____

_____

_____

_____

_____

_____

_____

_____

_____

_____

"To restrain grief, to inhibit it, to bottle it up, is to fail to use one of God's means for eliminating the pressure of sorrow."

– Norman Vincent Peale

HEARTACHES

I used to believe that love had to be hard work. Because of that belief, I was attracted to men that liked to put me to work. I was always busy making sure that their every need was met. It was like I was unconsciously telling them, "Look, I'll hold down the fort while you go out and do what boys do. I'll be here, working on myself when you need me. And don't worry, I'm a strong and independent woman and I'll never need you to compromise." Unfortunately, overtime this dating routine wore down my confidence and my belief that I could have a healthy relationship.

After a few heartbreaks, I did finally realize that by putting these men on a pedestal and denying my own needs that I was destroying myself. I became what we call, sick and tired of being sick and tired. I was done with giving myself away emotionally and even physically to a man who was clearly not fully invested in me. I needed some time to heal my once optimistic heart.

It was one year. I took a well-deserved 12-month break from men. You may think that's not a big deal for a woman in her 20s but remember, whether good or bad, I was used to always being in a relationship with someone. This break meant no dating, no movies, no dinner and definitely no exchange of phone numbers that could succumb to a late night booty call. A full break. I had to get content with being 'with' myself and not feeling insecure thinking that I was 'by' myself. Instead, I took on God as my man. I know it sounds silly but, God and I started dating!

We would attend bible study and church together weekly. I found myself waking up at 5 a.m. to read His word, with Him. If I couldn't fall asleep in the evening, I would call on Him, in prayer. There, in one year of all of the very early mornings and late nights, I found His presence. It was refreshing and safe. It became effortless. I didn't have to work for His love. I could let go and show God all my scars and weaknesses and He didn't leave. Instead, God began to restore me and became my source of endless love.

I also discovered the gift of gospel music. I stumbled upon Yolanda Adams and Fred Hammond. They are incredible artists and are fully anointed in their craft. When I played their music, I was transported to a place of worship, joy and gratitude. I was a seeker and I found exactly what I needed at that time which was, a solid spirit of faith. And when I became strong in myself again, I told God that I was ready for love. Only this time, with an earthly man.

Almost 5 years later, God sent him to me. Now, even in those years waiting patiently on God, I was not actively looking for this man. It was quite the exact opposite when he showed up in my life. My older sister knew a handsome man that she worked with and wanted to set me up on a blind date with him. Handsome? My older sister was in her 30s at the time. Who under the age of 65 uses the term, handsome? It took another 3 months for her to convince me. My denial that he could be the one was so real that on our so-called blind date, I brought along my older sister, her son, my younger sister and her boyfriend. You could tell that I was not interested in dating just anyone, I was waiting on God to send me the love of my life.

A few weeks later, he invited me to his friend's birthday party and we did meet again to have our official first date. Again, my family escorted me there and this time left soon after they arrived to allow us to get to know each other better. This time, without their help. Well, we continued to date. We broke up, twice. We got back together. Now after being inseparable for 4 years, I was engaged to marry this man that I truly loved and I knew who truly loved me. I only knew this because this time, I didn't hopelessly give myself away. I asked for what I needed.

So, you may be wondering if God answered my love prayer with the love of my life, then why am I lying on the floor of the bathroom in the master bedroom of the new home that I just bought with my now fiancé. Well, do you remember when Hurricane Katrina hit in 2005? According to the National Geographic, it was comparatively one of the most costly and deadly hurricanes, with 120 mph winds and subsequent flooding, it took the lives of over 1,200 people. The coastal states of Mississippi and Louisiana took a beating from the storm as it made its way up through the Gulf of Mexico. New Orleans, which was the most populous city in Louisiana, was estimated to be 80% under water only 1 day after it got hit. It was a massive devastation.

Along with many others around the country, my fiancé was a passionate professional that felt a strong calling to be a part one of the countless relief teams that would step in to help the victims restore their lives. He didn't hesitate. He signed an 8-month contract that would assist in rebuilding the apartment homes in the low income wards of New Orleans. I knew he was stepping up and into a role that was much needed at the time. What I didn't realize that only after a few months of moving into our new abode, that I would in essence, be living there alone.

My then fiancé would be traveling back and forth from our home in Atlanta to work in New Orleans on a weekly basis. Essentially, he would leave on an airplane every Monday morning and return every Thursday night for the next 8 months. No big deal, right? I convinced myself that I was young, adaptable and this would not be a difficult task. In spite of everything, I used to be one of the most independent women that I knew. I could keep myself busy with the setting up of my new home and I had a wedding to plan. Piece of cake!

For the first 3 months, I got up early at the start of every week to take him to the train station and I would eagerly make my way back to the station each Thursday evening to pick him up on time. Between the countless meetings of planning and working with the local contractors, he always had a lot on his plate when he was there. He was challenged to maximize his hours during the shorter work week and didn't really have a lot of time to spend on the phone listening to my decorating or wedding ideas. He was literally helping people restore all that they had lost in their lives. The loss of dry clothes, family pictures, warm blankets, and some lost their loved ones. Even still, like any sympathetic fiancé would do, I checked in throughout the day to see how things were coming along. I was there supporting him from the sidelines.

I couldn't dare complain. But, you do the math, 5 more months in this quasi long distance relationship and my old insecurities started taking over. I'd been in long distance relationships before and no matter how much love there is between the two of you, the distance seems to grow each time the other person leaves. It always felt like by the time you've reconnected, it is time for someone to go home. Well, my home became a dark and empty space. The greater problem was that I didn't let him know and I didn't let anyone else know how miserable I was becoming.

While my fiancé was helping those who suffered from one of the largest hurricanes in Louisiana, I was at home in Georgia, facing one of the biggest emotional storms of my life. My patience had worn thin and my enthusiasm was diminished. The sensitive baggage of my past resurfaced with feelings of elevated uncertainty and a deep sense of rejection flooded my self-esteem. I thought I had conquered that old thought pattern a long time ago. Unfortunately, it was back and it was bigger than before. I began to question my fiance's love for me. I became especially suspicious of the women that he worked with. I was completely terrified that I wasn't enough to keep this man in my life.

The dams that I was building around my facade of happiness were broken open. I blindly allowed my emotions get the best of me. Of course looking back now, it is no surprise that I had let life get busy and by focusing on the doubt in my head, I had neglected the practices of prayer and spending time with God. These practices healed me and sustained me when I was feeling weak and will continue to restore me for the rest of my life. My soul announced that I am more than me. That means, I am more than an independent women and a soon-to-be wife!

"Give God everything that you are NOT. Stop trying to give God everything you THINK you are. His strength is in our weakness!!"

– Joyce Meyer

FAITH

I have always said, that if I could have any super power in the world, it would be to have enough faith to move mountains. Just imagine that all you have to do is believe. Your belief could be a small as a mustard seed and no matter how big your enemy was, poof, they would be eliminated by your faith alone. You can laugh or disagree and say, that having faith is a weak power. You might say why not the amazing ability to fly? Run at lightning speed? Or how about becoming completely invisible, with the ability to spy on any person in the world?!? Nah! Faith to me, exceeds them all! In reality, we are not superheroes, however, we do have the super power to see in the absence of proof. We're all born with this power. Too bad that as we've aged and gained more life experiences, many of us stop engaging in this authority and even worse, have forgotten that it was ever there!

When I was a young girl, you could say that I was building a strong faith. I had a lot of things that I wanted to have in my life and many were things that I hadn't yet seen. It wasn't until my late teenage years that I began to have a real spiritual yearning to be closer to a higher power. For me, that higher power was God. Besides the very few adolescent teachings, I didn't really know who He was. I just knew I wanted to worship and spend time with Him. I could visualize myself sitting in one of the pews of a gorgeous cathedral with the bright afternoon sun streaming through the stained glass windows. In my imagination, I could even hear an angelic choir singing as I sat in the presence of God.

Regardless of my imagination, what I was really looking for was a greater sense of self and purpose in my young world. I began to feel a calling from God over my life. He was calling me to seek Him. I knew somewhere inside, that because of my lack of my biblical understanding, it would be my faith that would bring me solace. It would also bring me something that I had been earnestly longing for as a young girl, a real father figure.

It would be one day around the age of 19, that my same sister who later introduced me to my now husband, invited me to her church. I innocently accepted. It was a small church and I don't even remember what denomination it was. I do remember, that they were very conservative and that my sister stopped wearing make-up and pants for a short period. At the time, I was living a typical young adult life. I loved to play music and go to parties with my friends. We were out of High School and it felt like I was being a real adult! I had no idea that God was waiting for me around the corner.

"What do I wear?" I asked her cluelessly. "Just come as you are", she said. "Ok!" I naively responded.

So, it was a hot summer's day and I arrived in my cut off jean shorts that landed about 3 inches above the knee and one of my favorite t-shirts. Come as you are? I don't think so. Instantly, I could feel the looks of judgement and as sense the pity of the churchgoers as I walked through the doors of the church. I quickly found a seat in the closest pew. There, past the seemingly wall of shame, stood an Apostle. He was a very tall white man that stood out amongst the African American congregation. My sister mentioned to me that he was a prolific preacher with healing capabilities. All the reason I wanted to be there.

After promptly securing my seat, I noticed further down in the opposite pew that there were a few other girls sitting there that resembled me. They were youthful, dressed inappropriately and looked a little embarrassed to be there. Thinking back now, I never did ask my sister if her pastor summoned the parishioners to invite all the young and wild women they knew to church that Sunday. You know, the Misses who needed to be rescued from themselves. I understand now that it was done out of love so I absolutely have no hard feelings toward the church's behavior or my sister for inviting me.

The Apostle preached and made the alter call. For those, who have never been in a black church or a church at all, there's a significant moment at the end of the sermon when the pastor will call you to come to the front of the church if you want to be saved. If you are a sinner, then you need to be saved. If you don't want to remain a sinner, then go to the front of the church and the pastor will help guide you to everlasting life. If you don't give your life to God, then you will go to hell. Who wants that? I knew I didn't want to go the hell and I wanted to be saved but there was a mysterious fear that locked my feet to the floor. Getting up was the hardest part.

He extended the invitation again and this time specifically to the young women visitors. I had brought a friend with me and she and I looked at each other and I was the only one of us to stand up and make my way down the aisle. I just knew that she would follow my lead, but she never did. She stayed seated. I was scared yet, I felt brave. I was not even sure what was going to happen once I got there. It was like having an outer body experience walking down the aisle. My feet took over my fear and I finally arrived at the alter standing alongside the other gutsy girls. We lined up in a row facing the Apostle.

I can recall the slight awe of the church members when the Apostle asked us to raise our hands toward the ceiling and to recite a prayer. The girls looked as confused and as nervous as I was. I joined them in their uncertainty, raised my hands but with a lingering unbelief. The Apostle stood in front of the first girl and cupped her head into his hands. As he passionately prayed out loud for her. Her knees began to buckle and she fell to the ground. "Wow! He is magical!" I thought. He kept moving to the next girl and did the same and she too fell onto the ground. I had never seen what many Christians call, 'catching the Holy Spirit'. The girls were crying, almost in relief that they will not be beckoned to Hell.

The church became loud with organ music while the members watching from the pews began crying out loud to God and thanking Him for His saving grace. In the presence of all that energy, I recall telling myself that I was not going to fall to the ground. When the Apostle approached me and cupped my head and began to pray, just as I had thought, I didn't fall to the ground. I felt vulnerable and slightly embarrassed. Instead, I politely thanked him for praying for me and started to return to my seat.

As I turned away and headed back down the aisle, he pulled out a white handkerchief from his coat pocket as to majestically make me disappear. Instead, he gently dashed the back of my head with it and I immediately fell to the ground. Unhurt yet, unable to get up, I felt the presence of God over my life. He was telling me to bring Him all of my pain and anguish. As a feeling of peace consumed me, I too began to cry. The Apostle handed me the handkerchief and helped me back to my feet so I could return to where I was seated. My friend sat there in astonishment. I too was astounded by what had just happened. I knew that my life would never be the same after that day. And it wasn't. God became real in my life!

I kept that bright white handkerchief which eventually faded into a beige cloth over the years. However, when feelings of doubt or unbelief would creep in, I would find it and hold it my hand and reflect on that day when God came into my life. The Lord came into my life through the Apostle and became my personal Savior that day. I will never let myself forget that there is a greater power looking after me. God can present Himself to you too when you least expect it. If you don't believe me, ask Him to help your unbelief.

Over a decade later, I had a profound and vivid dream that I was flying free in sky without the assistance of a parachute, aide of wings or even the benefit of being inside of a plane. I flew without restrictions above this great landscape without a cloud in the sky. I was free. It was like I was an eagle effortlessly soaring above on a very clear and bright sunny day. Beneath me was a huge range of mountains. I never knew the specific location but it felt similar to the never ending horizon above the Grand Canyon.

I was very high in elevation and full of incredible joy and bliss. The pleasant feelings that I experienced were so overwhelming that I couldn't stop laughing and smiling. Someone was with me. I heard a voice say firmly, "I am here with you." In that that moment, I recognized His voice and I knew that I was with God. In this dream, He was allowing me to dance in the sky with Him.

Then quickly, I began to descend down toward what felt like a valley below. I was flying really fast and dipping down at a rapid rate. I started to feel a little concerned. More fear came over me, as the once wide open blue and sunny sky became a dark and wooded forest on both sides of me. Still flying at a very fast speed, I looked back and could clearly see behind me that the sun was shining at the beginning of the wooded path where I had entered. As I looked forward, my vision became very blurry and I remember feeling a great sense of doubt and confusion. I would look back, it was clear with a bright opening and again, when I looked forward, the path was not clear. I wanted to stop flying. No longer soaring high, I could now see the ground below, parallel to my body. I started to put my feet down toward the ground so that I could walk, when God startled me and spoke again saying, "I am STILL here with you!" I trusted his voice and I knew in that moment that he was there with me. I pulled my feet back up and continued to fly through this mysterious dark path down inside of the valley.

After I awoke, I was refreshed with a new hope. With elation, I called all of my family and told them about my dream. I shared how God was with me in the light moments and God was still there with me in my dark moments. He is ever present in our lives!! You may not believe in God but you may be a seeker of a higher power. Ask, and it **shall** be given **you**; **seek**, and ye **shall find**; knock, and it **shall** be opened unto **you**: For every one that asketh receiveth; and he that seeketh, findeth; and to him that knocketh it **shall** be opened. (Matthew 7:7-8). God is here for me and he is here for you too!

I like to mention that not I'm not a follower of a religion and the dogma that may come along with it. I am not even dismissing those who are religious. I am only stating that I believe in inclusion, not a further separation based on worshipping differences. However, I challenge those who do not have a religion to find a power bigger than yourself. Even as an atheist, you can study nature and you will see how our natural surroundings work within a divine flow. There's a constant change along with a familiar dance that occurs within nature and without man's assistance. Study that! We can continuously seek to ask and learn from everything around us and trust that there's a greater force always waiting there to assist us!

My Praying Tree, a poem by Jacquie M. Dumas (my maternal great aunt)
I placed my arms
'round my old pine tree
For the world that day
Had been cruel to me.
I raised my eyes
To the highest hill
And cried, "Dear Lord
I need you still."
I looked up where
The needles swayed
And once again
I softly prayed.
That the crusty vigor
Of my praying tree
Would somehow magically
Strengthen me.
As I leaned against
That old gray pine
I felt God's presence
Close to mine.
I headed home
And my heart was free
For I'd found solace
At my praying tree.

The next pages have been reserved for you to lay your burdens down. Have you've been holding on to a doubt for so long that it's become the truth? We all have wounds and disappointments that do not need to be carried throughout our lives. We have permission to give them over to a higher power.

Ask yourself the following questions,

What areas in your life are dark, unclear and need more light?

What in your life could use more peace for restoration?

Write them down and leave them here!

Journal Entry
Date:____

_____

_____

_____

_____

_____

_____

_____

_____

_____

_____

_____

_____

_____

_____

_____

_____

_____

_____

_____

_____

_____

Journal Entry
Date:____

_____

_____

_____

_____

_____

_____

_____

_____

_____

_____

_____

_____

_____

_____

_____

_____

_____

_____

_____

_____

Journal Entry
Date:_____

Journal Entry
Date:___

_____

_____

_____

_____

_____

_____

_____

_____

_____

_____

_____

_____

_____

_____

_____

_____

_____

_____

_____

_____

_____

Journal Entry
Date:____

_____

_____

_____

_____

_____

_____

_____

_____

_____

_____

_____

_____

_____

_____

_____

_____

_____

_____

_____

Journal Entry
Date:___

_____

_____

_____

_____

_____

_____

_____

_____

_____

_____

_____

_____

_____

_____

_____

_____

_____

Journal Entry
Date:____

_____

_____

_____

_____

_____

_____

_____

_____

_____

_____

_____

_____

_____

_____

_____

_____

_____

_____

_____

Journal Entry
Date:___

_____

_____

_____

_____

_____

_____

_____

_____

_____

_____

_____

_____

_____

_____

_____

_____

_____

_____

_____

_____

Journal Entry
Date:____

*"We must be willing to let go of the life that we planned
so as to have the life that is waiting for us!"*

- Joseph Campbell

AFFIRMATIONS

Currently, most people purchase their books by scrolling on a phone or a tablet without ever having to leave the comfort their home. I get it. We're all too busy these days. You have to make an extra effort to get in the car and drive to a store to potentially find and buy a new book. However, I used to enjoy the hunt for the next inspiration at the bookstore. I rarely went with a specific book in mind. I only went with a topic of concentration that most interested me and that was the self-help section.

You could find me patiently lingering up and down the aisles of this genre, perusing the titles that would catch my eye. During one of my successful book hunts, I stumbled upon The Dynamic Laws of Prosperity. This book found me. I was young, living on my own and I was seeking ways to increase my income. I wanted to earn money honestly and independently. So, of course, I bought the book.

I naively thought prosperity laws were only going to teach me step by step how to make money and save money. Nope. It is more than that. Prosperity is about more than just having more money. It's about having good health, peace of mind and the confidence that you will receive the desires of your heart. The author, Catherine Ponder, shares in great detail of how prosperity is a mindset, a discipline in developing your inner self to attract all that God and the universe wants to bring to you and it all starts with a declaration. This is where my love for affirmations was discovered.

An affirmation allows us the power to transform our lives simply by being our best cheerleader every day! It is then that you can activate the spiritual laws that are always around us. Ponder says the law of laws applies to us all. Whether we are Christians, Hindus or Buddhist, who believe that we will reap what we sow. Maybe, we are scientists that believe factually, that for every action, there is a reaction. Even those who are considered modern day philosophers, agree with Emerson, that the greatest law is declared, as the law of compensation.

I know who told you that you couldn't be prosperous… it was you! Even if it was someone else who told us first, we've internalized their words as our own belief thereafter. We all have internal conversations with ourselves constantly and we tend to live out in reality what we tell ourselves every day. Words have a great purpose in our lives. However, they can have a life of their own and whether spoken out loud or inside of our heads, they become seeds that begin to sprout, grow and define our future. If you speak or write positively, the words will grow like beautiful wild flowers. The opposite does exist too. If you are always negative in your thoughts or words to yourself and to others, then they will be become like weeds, stealing the nutrients from the soil so that nothing fruitful can grow.

In the Bible, Proverbs 18:21 says, "death and life are in the power of the tongue." In other words, what we speak has the power to blossom into healing and love in our lives or can equally drown our lives into sadness and sickness. So, what have you been telling yourself lately? Believe it or not, people can tell. Our bodies and life experiences become a mirror and reflect our most inner thoughts and beliefs. For instance, disease can stem from our own dis-ease with something that has happened or yet, that we fear will happen. There are mental patterns that create problems in our bodies and it does respond with a physiological reaction to what we tell ourselves. T.D. Jakes says we will eventually become what we talk about.

In one of my very favorite books, "You Can Heal Your Life, the author, Louise Hay explains that there is a probable cause for every illness and by creating a new thought pattern or an affirmation, we can begin to heal our lives. Cancer, for example may stem from a deep hurt or long standing resentment that is eating away at the self. Even problems like arthritis has a probable cause stemmed from feeling unloved or criticized. By integrating a new thought to forgive, and with the release of the past, while loving and approving of your present self, the healing process can begin. This is not to say that traditional medicine cannot heal our physical bodies, but there is a correlation between the mind and body in which a new thought pattern can be used as a supplement or a booster to healing the root cause of the discord between the two.

By claiming a new self-affirmation of, "I see others with love and I love and approve of myself", we can attract a more loving behavior toward ourselves. In addition, we can become empowered by our own experiences so that we can heal from the consequences of the negative chatter. You can change. Yes, you can change. I thought of an acronym for you to remember, R-A-C-E-S. Remember, we are each running our own race to a life of wholeness.

R = Release: Release all old fears, beliefs and suggestions that you are not worthy of what you want. Forgive yourself and others from your past.

Affirmation Alert! You can now say, "I forgive myself. I enjoy practicing my new mental skills!"

A = Awareness: Start noticing what you are telling others and yourself each day. If it's negative, change it.

Affirmation Alert! You can now say, "The answers within me come to my awareness with ease!"

C = Control: There's really not much that we can control around us. Start conversations where you can control a new attitude as if the glass is half full. Look for scriptures or quotes that you can use and meditate on as daily affirmations to stay positive.

Affirmation Alert! You can now say, "I am healthy, whole and complete!"

E = Expand: Start reading everything that you find interesting or helpful. There are endless self-help audio books, podcasts, and resources that can help you expand your knowledge on managing relationships, wealth and health.

Affirmation Alert! You can now say, "The gateway to wisdom and knowledge are open to me!"

S = See: Visualize yourself succeeding. It is okay to start small. Clean up an area in your home that you've been ignoring. Have you been putting off getting rid of the items that no longer fit you or your family? You are now making room for new and there is always someone else in your community that needs them! By showing up for yourself with the little things, you will begin to trust yourself to show up for the big things that you will want to do.

Affirmation Alert! You can now say, "I deserve the best and I accept it now!"

To this day, whenever I hear myself having negative thoughts and words, I pull out a notebook and start reading and writing affirmations. Get committed to changing your thoughts and see how it unfolds in your life. We can start now by changing how we communicate with ourselves. It is not super easy at first but, it does get easier. Remember, nothing worth keeping comes without a little effort on our part. Also, remember, it takes time to move out of a current situation. So, focus. Communicate what you want to others and to yourself and you will begin to attract it! Life is simple. You get what you give. Let's start now!

Affirmation Alert! You can now say, "I now allow great love to flow to the surface and fill my heart, body and mind. Please radiate from me in all directions and return back to me multiplied!"

"Argue for your limitations and you get to keep them."

- Elizabeth Gilbert quoting Richard Bach

The next pages have been reserved for you to write and create affirmations for yourself. You can read them daily or multiple times a day. Take a break from your social media accounts and write declarations for your life. Each day or each night, you can read back over them. You will begin to feel the positive energy of self-love building up in your life.

If you are not sure where to find inspiration for your affirmations, you can start with a Bible, a poem, a Sanskrit or even an inspirational song.

Start seeing and saying how the glass is half full. Get ready, get set, go!

Journal Entry
Date:____

_____

_____

_____

_____

_____

_____

_____

_____

_____

_____

_____

_____

_____

_____

_____

_____

_____

_____

Journal Entry
Date:____

_____

_____

_____

_____

_____

_____

_____

_____

_____

_____

_____

_____

_____

_____

_____

_____

_____

_____

_____

_____

Journal Entry

Date:____

Journal Entry
Date:____

_____

_____

_____

_____

_____

_____

_____

_____

_____

_____

_____

_____

_____

_____

_____

_____

_____

_____

Journal Entry
Date:____

Journal Entry
Date:____

_____

_____

_____

_____

_____

_____

_____

_____

_____

_____

_____

_____

_____

_____

_____

_____

_____

_____

Journal Entry

Date:____

_____

_____

_____

_____

_____

_____

_____

_____

_____

_____

_____

_____

_____

_____

_____

_____

_____

_____

Journal Entry
Date:____

_____

_____

_____

_____

_____

_____

_____

_____

_____

_____

_____

_____

_____

_____

_____

_____

_____

_____

_____

*"We need to be broken open in order for the
light of God to shine through."*

– Kim Pothier

THE SECOND BREAK

It would be close to 11 years later that I would find myself being emotionally split open again on the same bathroom floor. Only this time, I wasn't there alone. My husband was there as a moral support, comforting me and telling me to grieve through a small opening of the door. I had just waited over 15 minutes outside of the downstairs' bathroom for my mother, this once stocky ex-Marine, currently more like a shrinking size 2, to give me permission to enter the bathroom and aid her off of the toilet. With an inability to stand independently, she needed the assistance of her adult child. This evening that would be me. She was very grateful for the help but was vulnerable. She lost her independence and her pride hurt deep down, just like the Cancer that was attacking her ailing body. I tried not to mimic her vulnerability but tonight was different. I was feeling overwhelmed with a sadness that I could no longer deny and so I allowed that emotional pain to break me wide open once again.

My mother had been diagnosed with stage 4 cervical cancer and she didn't deserve to see my defeat reflected back to her. She agreed to the chemotherapy and radiation treatments and was doing very well until her body had become too weak to move at the pace that her free lifestyle was accustomed to. The treatment's side effects left her with neuropathy in her feet and it had been almost a year since she walked on her own. In recent months she wasn't strong even enough to use her walker without stumbling and losing her balance.

It would be one day when my older sister needed a much-deserved care giver break that my mom packed some things and stayed at my house for a few days. My mother seemed weaker and more fragile during this visit. It was a struggle for me seeing her once strong physical body become so weak. I stayed positive and gentle with her. I tried to keep her spirits high. I wanted to pamper her. I enjoyed playing her inspirational music and painting her fingernails in a bright melon color that she liked.

It wasn't until the last months of her life that she had become embarrassed about having to physically rely on others to help complete what were once simple daily tasks of self-care. As a matter of fact, my mom sought and worked very hard to achieve a simple and humble life. She created a life that would afford her peace of mind and most importantly, independence. I believe that it was the childlike look and blameless smile that she gave me that night as I tucked her comfortably into bed that sent me straight to my knees when I finally reached my upstairs bathroom.

Her innocent look had unmasked my poise and by acknowledging my greatest fear that I would lose her, I broke down. Every tear that fell from my eyes started out as an unspoken prayer to God. They soon transformed into a plea for her healing and quickly escalated into a ferocious battle cry for her life.

Why God?

Why God??

Why God!?!

Why have you taken the use of her legs? Did you forget her nickname is Bebop? She uses her legs to bring the joy of music into her life. She loves dancing to her favorite Motown songs and in her youth was voted Best Dancer in High School. She is an introvert until her favorite song comes on and then she becomes a full-fledged dancing machine! I know you didn't forget watching her dance at the reception of my wedding and the sheer elation that emanated from every pore in her body. She is pure beauty in motion! Did you forget that I promised her a dancing party once she gets the use of her legs back?

I know you didn't forget how she uses her legs to sacrifice for her family. What about the miles that she would walk alongside my dad when they first got saved and gave their lives over to you? They didn't yet have a car but that didn't stop them and their two young children from getting to the church that was nearly 30 miles away. Of course you had strangers pick them up and take them most of the way, but it was their faith in you that they put their feet in motion.

I know you didn't forget, my first business acquisition as a child when I took over my brothers' newspaper routes. I bought my first BMX bike and was excited to become a young entrepreneur and make my own money. Well, you knew that I couldn't do it on my own. It was my mom that would get up early on the weekends to help me assemble the papers and even in the snow, she used her legs to ride bikes with me to make sure every customer had their Sunday paper. Or how about the times when she would jump on a bike to ride me to my softball practices when her car wouldn't start?

Why God, have you taken the focus from her eyes? She can no longer enjoy her favorite past time of reading. You have to remember that she is beyond an avid reader. It was once her greatest escape from the insanity of raising 7 active children. You could always find her sitting somewhere in a room, comfortably caught up in an exciting novel or biography. She's my walking encyclopedia!

Don't you remember all of the last minute book reports she helped us with? She would stay up all night reading the book that we forgot to read and give us the cliff notes in the morning. What about her brilliant way of always finding the perfect card for every occasion? How is she going to read the words to know they are exactly what her children and grandchildren needed to hear in that exact moment?

Why God, are you letting this disease defeat her? She is invincible! You know how much of a fighter she's always been. Why are taking away my mother, my rock, my sanctuary and my children's grandmother? Why do you need her up there? I need her here. We need her here. The world needs her here. What will we do without her, here? God let me cry out my pain and probe

Him with my hard questions. He knew that I would never allow myself to succumb to my feelings of desperation in front of her.

I'll never forget playing her favorite Sam Cooke songs by her bedside in the Hospice room during one of the last days of her life. Her last words to me were, "Joc, I've been in so much pain. You don't know how much pain I've been in." Of course I didn't know the depth of her pain, because she never complained. I responded, "I know. I'm so sorry, mom." She fought until her body couldn't fight anymore and God eventually won the battle. She no longer had to endure the pain; she just had to leave her earthly body to achieve her bliss. My mom was gifted the trophy of eternal life and I gained a guardian angel on May 27, 2018.

It was early evening and we were making baked ziti with Italian bread and red wine when the Hospice employees arrived to drop off my mom at my younger sister's home. They carried her on the hospital's stark white bedsheets and laid her on the specific turquoise blue velvet chair facing the glassy lake in front of the large picture windows. She didn't say a word. She had been in the house for less than 30 minutes when she took her last breath. Her dentures fell from the roof of her mouth and she was gone. Knowing that my mom didn't speak until she was nearly 4 years old, gave me an added comfort that she left this earth as quietly and peacefully as she had entered it.

She resembled a Leonardo da Vinci painting with her slight Mona Lisa-like smile. Her hands laid there naturally crossed over each other in her lap. The polish on her fingernails now chipped away with only flecks of the bright orange color still present. My mom left this earth in the presence of 5 out of the 7 of her adult children and all of her 7 grandkids. For me, it actually was a brilliant experience as she transcended from her physical body into the next dimension. I call her blessed.

"What the caterpillar calls the end of the
world, the master calls a butterfly."

– Richard Bach

I had to let my mom go from being in my life physically, yet in spirit, she always comes back to me. Whether it's as her beloved cardinals that visit my purple tree in my front yard or the sweet kindness of her voice that soothes my sadness when I replay her voicemails that I had intentionally saved. Her presence is always with me!

The next pages have been reserved for you to write a love letter(s) to someone or something that you have lost in your life. Go ahead and pour your heart out on the pages. Don't hold yourself back. Let your heart break open and accept every tear thereafter as the prayers for your renewed healing.

Journal Entry
Date:____

_____

_____

_____

_____

_____

_____

_____

_____

_____

_____

_____

_____

_____

_____

_____

_____

_____

Journal Entry

Date:____

Journal Entry
Date:____

_____

_____

_____

_____

_____

_____

_____

_____

_____

_____

_____

_____

_____

_____

_____

_____

_____

_____

_____

Journal Entry
Date:____

_____

_____

_____

_____

_____

_____

_____

_____

_____

_____

_____

_____

_____

_____

_____

_____

_____

_____

_____

_____

Journal Entry
Date:____

_____

_____

_____

_____

_____

_____

_____

_____

_____

_____

_____

_____

_____

_____

_____

_____

_____

Journal Entry
Date:____

_____

_____

_____

_____

_____

_____

_____

_____

_____

_____

_____

_____

_____

_____

_____

_____

_____

_____

Journal Entry
Date:____

_____

_____

_____

_____

_____

_____

_____

_____

_____

_____

_____

_____

_____

_____

_____

_____

_____

_____

_____

_____

Journal Entry
Date:____

_____

_____

_____

_____

_____

_____

_____

_____

_____

_____

_____

_____

_____

_____

_____

_____

_____

_____

_____

Journal Entry
Date:___

"No more busy work. No more hiding from success. Leave time, leave space, to grow. Now! Now! Not tomorrow!"

– Og Mandino

GET PRESENT

I magine with me for a moment that someone has given you a beautifully wrapped gift, for no reason at all. The box is large and covered tightly in luxurious wrapping paper with gold and purple silk bows. You've accepted this beautiful gift and never use the item inside because you're really not sure how it works. The very next moment, you receive the instructions on how it works. You loosely read them and you throw them in your favorite junk drawer. We all have one! Or, there are those people that take the gift put the instructions inside the box and put up somewhere far in your closet. You tell yourself, "That was a very nice gift, I'll figure out how to use it when I retire. After all, I'll have so much more time on my hands then."

What is the gift you ask?

It is the gift of being present and living in the now. I'm sure you've all heard or seen the popular quote, "The past is history, and the future is a mystery but today is the gift. That's why it's called the present!" Unfortunately, many people hear a meaningful quote like this and only admire it for a minute and never stop to apply it as an affirmation to slow the pace of our busy lives.

Many of our lives include having to endure waking up to an annoying alarm clock and after several snooze sessions, the rush of our multi-tasking schedules begin. We make the to-go cup of coffee, feed the dog, let out the dog, let in the dog. Wake up the children for school, if they haven't woken us up first and try not to strangle them as they ask to watch a mindless cartoon series for the 15th time. Help them get dressed, teeth brushed, hair combed and fed with some kind of nutritious breakfast. Only to turn right around and do the same for ourselves. Don't forget as you run out the door to… Those 3 dots are there to only emphasize the list of things that we tell ourselves that we have to do each day. However, the list can begin to feel endless and even daunting some days.

It can be overwhelming when that is only the first few hours of your day. You haven't even started your car to go to work yet and you've already received 5 more texts from your boss about some nonsense "fires" that need your help to put out today. You drop the kids off properly from the carpool lane, get on the highway to sit in traffic, only to remember that you left your coffee mug on the counter at home. Now, you must stop at the next drive through coffee joint that has a line of only 10 cars ahead of you. Great minds think alike, huh?

You are relieved to finally arrive at work, pull into the parking lot, and park the car to catch up on the 3 more texts or emails that you received on the ride in. Check your voicemails from the calls that came in after 7 p.m. last night and return a few phone calls before you leave your vehicle. Oops! You forgot to recheck your calendar and you receive a reminder on your phone that you have a meeting that starts in the next 15 minutes. Yikes! The rush of adrenaline perks you up and out of the car and speed walk to your office.

Perhaps you have the job that requires you to stand on your feet all day and also to be the first one there which typically for you is, 4:30 a.m. You didn't want the conceived luxurious career of sitting in an office all day. You're a hustler. Your morning consists of waking up before the sun and heading to your outdoor office where you have the bonus of being out in nature all day. Except unfortunately, for the next 3 weeks, your outdoor paradise will not reach more than 40 degrees Fahrenheit!

After multiple alarm clocks have ceased, you leave the house prepared. You're wearing layers of thermal clothing, two pairs of socks and waterproof boots. The trunk of your car is considered your cubical. It's where you keep your working necessities which consist of, a change of clothes, quality rain gear, snow gear and another pair of shoes and socks that you will change out at lunchtime. Your office supplies are portable and include, a laptop, a wireless printer, 3-4 portable chargers, insect repellant, sunscreen, hand warmers and a tool box full of miscellaneous gadgets that any handyman or DYIer would admire!

Exhausted yet? No? Oh, you know that you've got stamina, huh? Well, you can try to keep up with a never-ending list for years and you may not see any negative side effects but trust that they are coming. The precious years of your endurance will go by and you can begin to experience feeling burnt out in your day to day grind. You look up and realize that you've never stopped your career to have a stable relationship or start a family that doesn't have 4 legs.

I'm not trying to scare you into not to having an active work or family life. I am only asking you to get present each day. At least, once a day. The goal is to simply focus on what is here and now and that can become challenging to do with a list of ceaseless tasks. Ok, enough task talk. How do I receive the gift, you ask?

With one breath at a time.

Start by sitting quietly, it can be in the bathroom or in a quiet chair before you start your day. Instead of scrolling on your phone first thing in the morning, take a moment to get still and breathe. Breathe in and out of your nose for 5 minutes. If you won't allow yourself 5 minutes, then give yourself 3 minutes. By just breathing in and out of your nose, you are now present. Focus on each inhale, feel how your belly can expand and your lungs fill with up with rich oxygen. Now, focus on each exhale. Feel the air leaving your lungs and your belly button contracting back toward your spine. Keep doing this for the minutes you allot yourself and you are now present!

You can use this gift of breathing throughout the day as much as you'd like! The more you do it, the better it feels. There is nothing like being present for yourself. If you can do this at the beginning of every day and before beginning new tasks throughout the day, you will have more clarity and a sense of intention as you work to complete your responsibilities.

When you are present, you can breathe and look at others directly in the eye. How often do we talk to each other and get busy looking everywhere but at each other. You can breathe and really focus on what the other person is saying. You can even breathe and appreciate how the sun is shining through the window and how its presence is warming the skin on your face. Breathe and notice the people who smile back when you smile at them! Breathe, take a bite of your favorite piece of chocolate and sip your favorite wine or favorite tea.

Just remind yourself to breathe and you can gain access to the many privileges of being in the present, such as mindfulness, gratitude and intention at any time. What is limited are the 24 hours that we each are granted each day. We may think that we have the health and the fortitude to live a long life, however, we don't know that. We do know that all of our earthly bodies will expire one day. No one is promised tomorrow. So, enjoy every moment now. Right now!

"You do not need to leave your room. Remain sitting at your table and listen. Do not even listen, simply wait, be quiet, still and solitary. The world will freely offer itself to you to be unmasked, it has no choice, it will roll in ecstasy at your feet."

- Frank Kafka

Instead of writing to reflect on being present, take a break and get into nature. You need to do this without scrolling on your phone, without listening to music and without a companion. Go to a park and sit on a bench alone. Try sitting under a large tree. Or have a cup of coffee or tea and sit on your porch. Listen, watch and learn how nature flows with ease in your presence.

"To surrender is to yield to the next stage of your evolution."

– Reverend Michael Beckwith

SURRENDER

When my mom passed away, I leaned heavily on my faith and my self-help practices to help me gain some peace after losing her. Knowing that she was no longer in my physical life and knowing that my comforts were only temporary, I began seeking a higher place to rest my ongoing pain. I was looking for a greater state of awareness for managing my new grief, one that would require a new level of consciousness.

Why was it so hard to surrender this hurt? You could say that I had become a junkie, obsessed with creating a most improved version of myself. I was only focusing on the pleasures of achieving the outcomes of my practices and ignoring the value of time in the processes that got me there. Well, surrender doesn't require perfection and I needed a detox. Would that mean that I would have to stop the inner work that I began decades ago? In order to answer this question, I had to refrain from my old point of view that I had to lose something in order to gain the insight that surrender would bring. Ironically, it became my sacred place of receiving. As Jane Fonda said, "We're not meant to be perfect, we're meant to be whole."

What I'm always learning while practicing the art of surrender is that surrendering is staying present in the now, after the inner work is done. The effort that I am putting into my self-help practices is the same effort I need to surrender to them. As I start to get still and breathe, I become my faith, I become my affirmations and my healing is here, in this present moment. While surrendering to the search of my better self, I find in the meditations of my stillness, a greater sense of contentment with my imperfections. I find a fresh sense of self-acceptance.

It's funny how your mind will trick you into thinking that you cannot have more, with less. The more I get still and meditate, the less I hold on to the outcomes of my practices. The more I meditate in my solitude, the more I want to connect with life and the living things around me. When my mind gets still and I listen closely to my heart, I no longer reject the traits that I once believed I that I inherited. Instead of judging my past, I've embraced that no matter how much I've evolved, I will always be flawed. In fact, it's become very clear that my imperfections are imperative to my authentic human experience.

As surrender becomes a new normal in your life, there is still a need for an ongoing dedication to continue to trust yourself in the processes and not the outcomes. It's finding the daily balance of showing up for yourself and then releasing all expectations of your practices. Some say, "Let go and let God!" You will find that there's a great flow of power when you set an intention and leave plenty of room for an uncompromising grace to show up and show out.

An additional wellness practice that I've committed to incorporating into my life is Hatha Yoga. This practice of poses and breathing are combined to gently realign your body, mind and spirit. It has become an essential tool in connecting my intentional effort with the ethereal ease to the physical, mental and spiritual aspects of my life. Outside, I'm relying on my physical body to hold the postures. While inside, my thoughts become quiet and my focus is on my breath. In this stillness of my mind, I am very present and I am very alive.

Most people think that they are not in good enough shape to do it. The opposite is quite true. Of course, you will always want to check in with your doctor before performing new exercises. However, if you are interested, a guided yoga class will always provide you with the proper modifications from the class instructors. Yes, Yoga will meet you where you are. Yoga is for children, seniors, the disabled and especially both genetically and mentally inflexible people.

Your body will love Yoga. According to the Chopra Center, Yoga is a profound practice that can heal your body. Yoga can reduce your blood pressure and the production of cortisol. The poses improve the flow of the lymphatic system that helps us fight infection and toxins in the body. There is only one requirement to receive the full benefits and experience of the postures, you must breathe. The breath brings you present and also scientifically adds oxygen to your cells. Hello body!

Our minds will love Yoga. Our conscious mind is a powerful thing. It holds our memories, our emotions and our ego. However, we should not give it full authority over our lives, as it is here to serve as a mere helper, not the lead. Through Yoga's many diverse poses, we can relieve our cerebral ails such as, anger, anxiety and chronic pain. Most importantly, having a regular Yoga practice brings a greater sense of peace to one's mind. As it reminds us to be present in our bodies and work through any present discomforts that the mind cannot fix. If there is no current pain, I will dedicate my practice to someone else who may be hurting and I will choose to be a symbolic beacon of light, by sending an energy of love to those who are in need.

Yes, our souls love Yoga. We are no longer just our bodies and our minds. We are of spirit and the deep light within us is our soul. Although, our spirit can be muddled with the mind and the body at times, with a regular Yoga practice, we can learn to trust our spirit and increase its focus within us. Postures for clearing the self-doubt and quieting the inner nagging voice will help us expose those dark and depleting insecurities that will pop up from time to time. With Yoga, our spirit can be trusted to further develop our intuition and become one of our greatest companions to lead us in this life!

Dr. Wayne Dyer – "Surrender is where your body and your mind aren't running the show and you move into intent."

The next pages are reserved for your flaws that you want accept or even ones that you have already overcome. It's so precious to be vulnerable with yourself and accept yourself with your conceived imperfections.

Shine a light to them so they are no longer a dark secret or shameful.

Be gentle with yourself.

Remind yourself that you are having an authentic human experience!

Journal Entry
Date:____

_____

_____

_____

_____

_____

_____

_____

_____

_____

_____

_____

_____

_____

_____

_____

_____

_____

_____

_____

Journal Entry
Date:___

_____

_____

_____

_____

_____

_____

_____

_____

_____

_____

_____

_____

_____

_____

_____

_____

_____

_____

Journal Entry
Date:____

_____

_____

_____

_____

_____

_____

_____

_____

_____

_____

_____

_____

_____

_____

_____

_____

_____

_____

_____

_____

Journal Entry
Date:____

_____

_____

_____

_____

_____

_____

_____

_____

_____

_____

_____

_____

_____

_____

_____

_____

Journal Entry
Date:____

_____

_____

_____

_____

_____

_____

_____

_____

_____

_____

_____

_____

_____

_____

_____

_____

_____

Journal Entry
Date:___

_____

_____

_____

_____

_____

_____

_____

_____

_____

_____

_____

_____

_____

_____

_____

_____

_____

Journal Entry
Date:____

_____

_____

_____

_____

_____

_____

_____

_____

_____

_____

_____

_____

_____

_____

_____

_____

_____

_____

Journal Entry
Date:____

_____

_____

_____

_____

_____

_____

_____

_____

_____

_____

_____

_____

_____

_____

_____

_____

_____

"Sat, chit, ananda. I am true existence. I am
true consciousness. I am true bliss!"

– Deepak Chopra

CONCLUSION: THE SURRENDERED LIFE

You can only manifest what you have inside. You are the commanding light of the universe which comes from God. I had to be broken open several times in order for this light to shine through. I am that old terracotta pot that was traditionally formed from raw, coarse clay that had water added to my life. Strained, to remove the dust. Drained, from the excess water and strained again to remove more dust and small rocks. I had to be rolled, pounded and protected. Finally, with the right consistency, I was molded and placed in the sunlight to be set. It is a formal process that can be done by hand. Whose hand are you letting mold you?

There are pots with small fractures, a little chip here and there and every once in a while, there's a real good crash. Are there chunks of your terracotta life still the floor where you left them? Or have you tried to glue them all back together again? Were you clever enough to just buy a new pot and hope the old one is never discovered. I had to stop hiding from my pain. I had to face it, comfort it and sit with it because I am more than it.

The surrendered life happens when you've done all the work in the self-help books. You've journaled and declared your affirmations regularly. You pray and worship. You have committed to a practice of being more centered and present in your daily life. You empathize and find others who celebrate you. You find a physical exercise that gets you present and strong in your body. You find ways to meditate and sit in stillness and you're getting better at cancelling the inner noise.

Now, you have to let it all go. You are more than your practices and your life is beckoned to evolve. Our greater self is calling! Can you hear you're your inner voice? Surrender to that inner knowing and trust that your guiding spirit will lead you to the path of the higher you! Ultimately, my spirit gave me permission to express a few critical moments of my life. I've shared the hurdles, the small glories and the tools that I've used to work through my anxiety and self-judgment. I still have more struggles, but I've been set free to share them all. Let your truth begin to set you free! Put aside the fear. Get to work. Laugh. Love. Cry. And do it all over again! Let's share and see how bright we can all shine together! You are more than you!

"Learn to ask for what you need and accept what is given."

– Mark Nepo

ACKNOWLEDGEMENTS

There is always inspiration in nature and in others that help us develop into who we are meant to be.

A heartfelt thank you to my parents, Jimmy Key and the late Barbara Key. Neither perfect yet, you both will remain as invaluable teachers in my life!

To my husband, Patrick Nelson and my children, Luke and Gabriel, you are my light in the dark places of this world. I love you to the moon and back and beyond each and every galaxy!

A special thanks to my proof readers, Jacqueline Perry & Adrienne Key.

Thank you to the following *sheroes* and *heroes* along the way:

Jesus Christ, Michael Beckwith, Lisa Bennett, Julia Cameron, Joseph Campbell, Dale Carnegie, Kyle Cease, Deepak Chopra, Dwayne Dyer, Elizabeth Gilbert, Steve Harvey, Louise Hay, Caleb Holland, Dr. Shirlene Holmes, Lewis Howes, T.D. Jakes, John Kelliher, Marsha Needham, Susan Mittleman, Norman Vincent Peale, Catherine Ponder, Kim Pothier, Eckhart Tolle, Janet Urban, Iyanla Vanzant, Doreen Virtue, Raphael G. Warnock, Oprah Winfrey & Lillie Young.

I send a special prayer of healing to all of the Hurricane Katrina families that were and are still impacted by its devastation.

Finally, I cannot forget to mention the immense amount of gratitude for my purple tree and the cardinals that visit me there.

Printed in the United States
By Bookmasters